Vegetarian Cookbook for Beginners

Easy and Delicious Recipes

Disclaimer

The ideas, concepts and opinions expressed in this book are intended to be used for educational purposes only. This book is provided with the understanding that the authors and publishers are not rendering medical advice of any kind, nor is this book intended to replace medical advice, nor to diagnose, prescribe or treat any disease, condition, illness or injury.

It is imperative that before beginning any diet or exercise program, you receive full medical clearance from a licensed physician. Author and publisher claim no responsibility to any person or entity for any liability, loss, or damage caused or alleged to be caused directly or indirectly as a result of the use, application or interpretation of the material in this book.

Summary – The Cookbook that Redefines Contemporary Vegetarian Cooking

There are many vegetarian cookbooks out on the market. What makes this cookbook stand out in particular is the wide range of fantastic simple recipes which don't require you to spend hours in the kitchen trying to cook the perfect meal for your family and friends.

There is a common misconception amongst many people today that vegetarian food and cooking is not real food or real cooking. However, if you go through the recipes in this cookbook you are bound to find some absolutely delicious recipes which will have even the most skeptical of people coming back for seconds.

Vegetarian cooking is an art which should be celebrated and in this current period of time when people are getting more stressed out due to their work and other stresses of daily life, it is imperative that we take the step to start eating healthy. Most of the time people don't know how to start eating vegetarian food or how to start cooking vegetarian food.

This cookbook is designed to target people who have just started a vegetarian diet and want uncomplicated, simple vegetarian recipes that are easy to make and extremely delicious when it comes to taste. This book is crammed with some of the most popular vegetarian dishes right now, which are extremely simple to make. This will ensure that you stay in touch with contemporary vegetarian cooking and also learn some new skills in the kitchen to enhance your cooking prowess and surprise your loved ones.

Some of the most well loved and healthiest vegetarian recipes are:

1. Whole Wheat Pancakes
2. Baked Asparagus
3. Ginger Veggie Stir-Fry
4. Kale Salad with Pomegranate and Maple Pecans
5. Toasted Garlic Bread

Vegetarian food is something which is gaining tremendous exposure in society today, and sooner rather than later, everyone will start shifting towards a healthier diet. It is your responsibility to look after the health of your family and yourself to ensure a brighter and healthier future. This vegetarian cookbook is designed to redefine contemporary vegetarian cooking and allow you to gain exposure to fundamental vegetarian recipes.

Contents

Introduction to Vegetarian Diet and Cooking

Vegetarian diet and cooking is the modern way to go about when it comes to eating healthy and cooking healthy. Most of the time, many people have the wrong idea when it comes to vegetarian cooking and diet and you are bound to hear things such as *"vegetarian food is boring"* or *"vegetarian food does not have enough taste in it"*.

The fact of the matter remains that the majority of the people who complain about vegetarian food and a vegetarian diet, do so because they misunderstand the overall concept of the vegetarian diet. It can be as a direct result of their thinking, since many people simply can't fathom the fact that you would prefer to eat something other than meat, which has for centuries been defined as the food of gladiators.

During the past quarter of a century, there has been a significant increase in the popularity of vegetarian food and now almost everyone you find is on a vegetarian diet. Most of them have switched due to health concerns, while others have done it, because it is the fashionable way and because everyone they know is doing it.

Whatever the cause is, we can't deny that society today has accepted vegetarian food and diet, as a healthier alternative and therefore we can safely assume that it is here to stay for good. So if you are beginner who has just switched onto a vegetarian diet, what better way than to learn a few of the classic vegetarian recipes for you to whip out the next time you host a party at your home and show your meat loving friends, what vegetarian food is all about.

A vegetarian diet typically includes core ingredients such as beans, grains, fruits, legumes and vegetables of course. There are literally thousands of delicious and tasty dishes you can make, when it comes to vegetarian cooking and you are bound to learn some of them in this cookbook. The following pages are sure to be an eye opener for you, so keep on reading.

Original Mouthwatering Vegetarian Recipes

Vegetarian food has grown in demand over the past few years, as people today encourage exercising and healthy dieting to promote a healthy lifestyle. If you are one of those people who have recently switched to a vegetarian diet, you may be looking for alternatives to scrumptious vegetarian food that will make your taste buds swell.

Vegetarian food has unfortunately been labeled by many people as boring food, with no taste and when it comes to cooking a form with no skill and expertise required. That can't be further from the mark if you tried and you will find some simply exquisite recipes in the following pages that will leave your friends and family drooling and asking for seconds!

There are tons of vegetarian recipes, which are bound to catch your fancy, but it is also important to take it slow and get your taste buds acclimatized with vegetarian food before you attempt some of the more complex recipes when it comes to preparing vegetarian food for friends and family.

Try some of the original mouthwatering recipes in the following pages and surprise everyone!

Vegetarian Recipes for a Wholesome Breakfast

Breakfast is widely considered to be one of the most important meals of the day. That does hold some truth as a great breakfast has the potential to revitalize you throughout the day. When you have switched to a vegetarian diet, it is imperative that you learn some vegetarian recipes for breakfast as well.

There is nothing better than having a nice fresh breakfast in the morning to give you a great start for the rest of the day. Vegetarian food allows you to get all the nutrition that your body requires and also keeps you fresh and wide awake till lunch time. You will start to notice the difference yourself once you learn a few of the recipes regarding vegetarian breakfast.

The following recipes are not complicated and require minimal preparation and cooking time, since time is of the essence during the early hours of the day. Let's be honest, no one likes to start the day spending a whole amount of time in the kitchen, and it is important to learn about recipes that require minimal effort from you but provide exceptional results in the end.

Have a go at these vegetarian recipes for a wholesome breakfast and make a bright start for a bright day. Every day!

German Potato Pancakes

Preparation Time: 25 minutes

Approximate Cooking Time: 6 minutes

Ready in: 45 minutes

Nutritional Value per Serving:

Calories: 283

Carbohydrates: 40.7 grams

Fats: 11 grams

Proteins: 6.8 grams

Cholesterol: 70 mg

Serving Size: Serves 6 people

Ingredients

6 peeled and shredded, medium potatoes

2 tbsp of flour

¼ tsp of pepper

¼ tsp of baking powder

¼ cup of vegetable oil

½ tsp of salt

½ cup of onion, finely chopped

Directions

Step 1: Take a big bowl and add the salt, pepper and baking powder in the bowl.

Step 2: Add the onions and potatoes to the bowl and mix them all.

Step 3: Place a large pan over medium heat and add the vegetable oil once the pan is hot.

Step 4: Drop the mixture of the potato into the pan in adequate batches according to your preference.

Step 5: Once in the pan, attempt to shape the mixture into flat shapes.

Step 6: Cook the pancake for 3 minutes on each side, so that it may get a nice brown color and crispy texture.

Step 7: Drain the pancakes on a paper towel to soak the oil out of them.

Step 8: Serve and enjoy German Potato Pancakes.

Baby Spinach Omelet

Preparation Time: 6 minutes

Approximate Cooking Time: 9 minutes

Ready in: 15 minutes

Nutritional Value per Serving:

Calories: 186

Carbohydrates: 2.8 grams

Fats: 12.3 grams

Proteins: 16.4 grams

Cholesterol: 430 mg

Serving Size: Serves 2 people

Ingredients

1 Cup of baby spinach leaves, torn

2 eggs

¼ tsp of onion powder

1 ½ tbsp of Parmesan cheese, grated

1/8 tsp of nutmeg, ground

Salt and Pepper for added taste

Directions

Step 1: Beat the 2 eggs thoroughly and pour them into a sizeable bowl.

Step 2: Add the Parmesan cheese and baby spinach and mix with the eggs.

Step 3: Add the nutmeg, pepper, and salt and onion powder into the mixture for seasoning.

Step 4: Place a small pan over medium and coat it with cooking spray.

Step 5: Add the mixture and cook for approximately 3 minutes, until the egg mixture is set partially.

Step 6: Continuing cooking the mixture for at least 3 more minutes and flip it from time to time with the help of a spatula.

Step 7: Lower the heat and keep cooking till you get your preferred result.

Step 8: Serve and enjoy Baby Spinach Omelet.

Whole Wheat Pancakes

Preparation Time: 20 minutes

Approximate Cooking Time: 30 minutes

Ready in: 50 minutes

Nutritional Value per Serving:

Calories: 548

Carbohydrates: 57.2 grams

Fats: 29.5 grams

Proteins: 17 grams

Cholesterol: 175 mg

Serving Size: Serves 5 people

Ingredients:

1/3 cup of wheat germ

1 cup of flour, whole wheat

2/3 cup of flour, all-purpose

1 ½ tsp of baking powder

1 tsp of salt

2 beaten eggs

½ tsp of baking soda

5 1/3 tbsp of butter, unsalted

2 tbsp of brown sugar

2 ½ cups of buttermilk

3 tbsp of butter, unsalted

Directions

Step 1: Take a large bowl or a food processor and the white flour, baking powder, whole wheat flour, baking soda, brown sugar, salt, and oats or wheat germ.

Step 2: Combine and mix them all together.

Step 3: Slice the butter into miniature pieces and add it to the mixture.

Step 4: Mix the butter until it reaches consistency.

Step 5: Add the eggs and buttermilk into the mixture by making a little well in the center.

Step 6: Thoroughly stir the liquid until it is well integrated.

Step 7: Place a skillet over medium heat and oil or 1 tbsp of butter for greasing the surface.

Step 8: Pour the mixture into the skillet and form it into pancake. Each pancake should be 4 inches in size.

Step 9: Flip the pancakes, once little bubbles start forming on its surface and cook for at least 2 minutes.

Step 10: Serve and enjoy Whole Wheat Pancakes.

Easy Broccoli Quiche

Preparation Time: 20 minutes

Approximate Cooking Time: 30 minutes

Ready in: 50 minutes

Nutritional Value per Serving:

Calories: 371

Carbohydrates: 21.5 grams

Fats: 24.9 grams

Proteins: 16.1 grams

Cholesterol: 179 mg

Serving Size: Serves 6 people

Ingredients

4 well beaten eggs

1 mined onion

2 tbsp of butter

1 ½ cups of milk

1 tsp of garlic, minced

1 tsp of salt

2 cups of fresh broccoli, chopped

1 tbsp of melted butter

1 ½ cups of mozzarella cheese, shredded

1 pie crust (9 inch), unbaked

½ tsp of black pepper

Directions

Step 1: Heat your oven to 175 degrees C (350 degrees F).

Step 2: Place a large skillet over medium heat to low heat and melt the butter.

Step 3: Add the garlic, broccoli and onions to the skillet.

Step 4: Cook the all the vegetables slowly until they turn soft, occasionally stir them.

Step 5: Spoon the vegetables into a crush and add a sprinkling of cheese over them.

Step 6: Mix the milk and eggs to the mixture and season them with salt and pepper.

Step 7: Add melted butter to the eggs and milk mixture and stir it.

Step 8: Pour the mixture of egg on top of the cheese and vegetables.

Step 9: Place them into the oven now and bake until the center is well set or for at least 30 minutes.

Step 10: Serve and enjoy the Broccoli Quiche.

Killer Tomato Bagel Sandwich

Preparation Time: 10 minutes

Approximate Cooking Time: 10 minutes

Ready in: 10 minutes

Nutritional Value per Serving:

Calories: 283

Carbohydrates: 40.7 grams

Fats: 11 grams

Proteins: 6.8 grams

Cholesterol: 70 mg

Serving Size: Serves 6 people

Ingredients

4 leaves of fresh basil

2 tbsp of cream cheese

1 toasted and split bagel

1 thinly sliced plum (roma) tomato

Directions

Step 1: Take the two halves of the bagel and spread them with some cream cheese.

Step 2: Add tomato slices over the top of the cream cheese.

Step 3: Sprinkle some salt and pepper for seasoning and taste over the top.

Step 4: Serve and enjoy the Tomato Bagel Sandwich.

Vegetarian Lunch Recipes for a Refreshing Afternoon Meal

If you ask most people, preparing a lunch time meal is extremely demanding, and you generally don't want to spend a lot of time in the kitchen creating a heavy meal. A vegetarian lunch time meal has to be simple and easy to make, yet deliver in taste and quality as well. When it comes to lunch, most people prefer their meals to be on the lighter side, since they don't want to consume something which will make them drowsy and lazy during the rest of the day.

The most obvious choice by many of these people is to have a nice vegetable lunch, which may include salads, or appetizers. A nice vegetarian lunch has got all the essential ingredients to produce a refreshing effect, and spark the sleepiest individual into life. However, you also don't want to spend a lot of time preparing a lunchtime meal for the family during the summer days, which is why preparing a vegetarian meal for lunch is the way to go.

The major hurdle you may have to face when preparing vegetarian dishes, are to make them appealing to the young ones, who are more than likely to put up a stern fight when it comes to vegetables. The following lunch time recipes are designed to take that factor into account, so you have nothing to worry about. So here are some of the best vegetarian lunch time recipes for a refreshing afternoon meal!

Baked Asparagus with Balsamic Butter Sauce

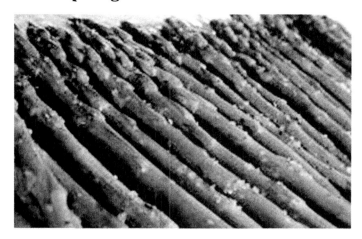

Preparation Time: 10 minutes

Approximate Cooking Time: 12 minutes

Ready in: 25 minutes

Nutritional Value per Serving:

Calories: 77

Carbohydrates: 4.9 grams

Fats: 5.9 grams

Proteins: 2.8 grams

Cholesterol: 15 mg

Serving Size: Serves 4 people

Ingredients:

Cooking Spray

1 trimmed bunch of fresh asparagus

2 tbsp of butter

1 tsp of balsamic vinegar

1 tbsp of soy sauce

Salt and Pepper for seasoning

Directions

Step 1: Set the heat in the oven to 200 degrees C (400 degrees F)

Step 2: Spread the asparagus on top of a baking sheet.

Step 3: Coat the asparagus with a sprinkling of cooking oil and add salt and pepper for seasoning.

Step 4: Put the asparagus in the oven and cook for approximately 12 minutes, or until it turns soft.

Step 5: Place a skillet over medium heat and melt the butter.

Step 6: Remove the skillet from the heat and add some balsamic vinegar and soy sauce to the skillet.

Step 7: Pour the mixture on top of the baked asparagus before serving.

Step 8: Serve and enjoy baked asparagus with balsamic butter sauce.

Spinach and Strawberry Salad

Preparation Time: 10 minutes

Ready in: 10 minutes

Nutritional Value per Serving:

Calories: 235

Carbohydrates: 22.8 grams

Fats: 15.9 grams

Proteins: 3.6 grams

Cholesterol: 69 mg

Serving Size: Serves 8 people

Ingredients:

½ cup of sugar, white

2 bunches of rinsed spinach, tear into small bite size pieces

¼ tsp of paprika

4 cups of strawberries, sliced

2 tbsp of sesame seeds

½ cup of vegetable oil

1 tbsp of poppy seeds

¼ cup of vinegar, white wine

Directions

Step 1: Throw some strawberries and spinach together in a bowl.

Step 2: Take another bowl and mix the paprika, sugar, poppy seeds, vinegar and oil together.

Step 3: Pour the entire mixture over the spinach and strawberries and ensure that it is coated evenly.

Step 4: Serve and enjoy the spinach and strawberry salad.

Vegetarian Chickpea Sandwich Filling

Preparation Time: 20 minutes

Ready in: 20 minutes

Nutritional Value per Serving:

Calories: 259

Carbohydrates: 43.5 grams

Fats: 5.8 grams

Proteins: 9.3 grams

Cholesterol: 2 mg

Serving Size: Serves 3 people

Ingredients:

1 tbsp of lemon juice

1 chopped stalk of celery

½ chopped onion

1 tsp of dill weed, dried

1 tbsp of mayonnaise

1 drained and rinsed can of garbanzo beans (19 oz)

Directions

Step 1: Rinse the chickpeas and drain them properly.

Step 2: Put the chickpeas into a mixing bowl of medium size and mash them. You may use a fork for mashing the chickpeas.

Step 3: Add onion, lemon juice, celery, dill, salt and pepper, and mayonnaise to the chickpeas.

Step 4: Mix them together by tossing around.

Step 5: Serve and enjoy the vegetarian chickpea sandwich filling.

Zucchini Herb Casserole

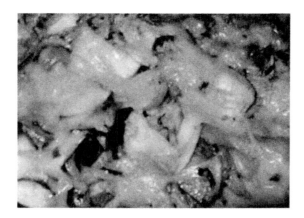

Preparation Time: 15 minutes

Approximate Cooking Time: 40 minutes

Ready in: 55 minutes

Nutritional Value per Serving:

Calories: 266

Carbohydrates: 16.5 grams

Fats: 17.5 grams

Proteins: 12.4 grams

Cholesterol: 40 mg

Serving Size: Serves 6 people

Ingredients:

2/3 cup of water

1/3 cup of long grain white rice, uncooked

½ tsp of basil

2 tbsp of vegetable oil

1 ¼ tsp of garlic salt

½ tsp of paprika

1 ½ pounds of cubed zucchini

1 clove of minced garlic

2 cups of Cheddar cheese, shredded sharp and divided

1 cup of green onions, sliced

½ tsp of dried oregano

1 ½ cups of chopped and seeded tomatoes

Directions

Step 1: Add water and rice together into a skillet and bring them up to a boil.

Step 2: Reduce the heat of the fire and cover the skillet.

Step 3: Let the rice and water simmer for approximately 20 minutes or until the rice turns tender.

Step 4: Turn the temperature in the oven to 175 degrees C (350 degrees F) and preheat.

Step 5: Get a casserole dish of about 1 ½ quart in size and grease it lightly.

Step 6: Place another skillet over medium heat and add garlic, green onions and zucchini to it.

Step 7: Mix all the components in the skillet and cook until they are tender or for approximately 5 minutes.

Step 8: Add oregano, paprika, basil and garlic salt for seasoning.

Step 9: Add these ingredients to the cooked rice and also add a cup of cheese and tomatoes to it.

Step 10: Mix them well and stir regularly until thoroughly cooked.

Step 11: Add the entire mixture into the lightly greased casserole dish and sprinkle some cheese on top for added flavor.

Step 12: Place the casserole dish into the oven and bake the dish uncovered for approximately 20 minutes, or till the cheese start to get bubbly or melts.

Toasted Garlic Bread

Preparation Time: 10 minutes

Approximate Cooking Time: 5 minutes

Ready in: 15 minutes

Nutritional Value per Serving:

Calories: 213

Carbohydrates: 23.4 grams

Fats: 10.1 grams

Proteins: 6.9 grams

Cholesterol: 22 mg

Serving Size: Serves 10 people

Ingredients:

5 tbsp of softened butter

1 tsp of dried oregano

1 loaf of Italian bread, 1 pound

2 cloves of crushed garlic

1 cup of mozzarella cheese, shredded

2 tsp of olive oil, extra virgin

Salt and pepper for seasoning and taste

Directions

Step 1: Heat a broiler beforehand.

Step 2: Take the bread and cut into slices which are about 1 – 2 inches thick.

Step 3: Take a small bowl and mix the oregano, olive oil, butter, salt, pepper and garlic.

Step 4: After preparing the mixture, spread it evenly on the slices of bread.

Step 5: Place the bread slices evenly on a baking sheet and broil until they turn slightly brown or for approximately 5 minutes.

Step 6: Check the slices at regular intervals to ensure that they are not burnt.

Step 7: Take the bread out after 5 minutes and some cheese over the top of the bread.

Step 8: Return the bread to the broiler and cook for a further 2 – 3 minutes or until the cheese is melted and brown in color.

Step 9: Serve and enjoy the toasted garlic bread.

Straightforward Vegetarian Recipes for a Romantic Dinner

Dinner time is a time where you often want to relax and have a good time with your family. It is the time of the day where you want to enjoy a nice meal with your special someone. A nice dinner meal holds the key to a perfect day, and invariably marks the end of a truly spectacular day. It is widely said that breakfast is the most important meal of the day, but for some people dinner takes even more priority over the other meals of the day, particularly if you are having people over for dinner.

When you are cooking vegetarian food for dinner, it is essential that you keep the theme of the dishes fairly straightforward and don't try to outdo yourself by attempting to cook something complex and sophisticated. When you are cooking with vegetables it is important not to overcook them, since the taste of burnt vegetables is not something you would ever want to experience.

The following vegetarian recipes for dinner are designed to help you cook an absolutely gorgeous meal that is fit to entertain anyone at your household and does not require you to take any cooking classes as well. Dinner time should be all about relaxation, family, and romance and the following recipes certainly tick all the important boxes.

Have fun cooking the vegetarian recipes for an extremely romantic dinner with the following meals, which are sure to earn you some rave reviews!

Grilled Potatoes and Onion

Preparation Time: 15 minutes

Approximate Cooking Time: 30 minutes

Ready in: 45 minutes

Nutritional Value per Serving:

Calories: 278

Carbohydrates: 40.1 grams

Fats: 11.8 grams

Proteins: 4.8 grams

Cholesterol: 31 mg

Serving Size: Serves 4 people

Ingredients:

4 sliced potatoes

1 tsp of black pepper, ground

4 tbsp of butter

1 tsp of salt

1 sliced red onion

Directions

Step 1: Place a grill over medium heat beforehand.

Step 2: Take aluminum foil and cut it into little pieces which can be used for wrapping the vegetables easily.

Step 3: Place the onion and potatoes in the middle of aluminum foil, grease with butter, and add a sprinkling of salt and pepper over the top.

Step 4: Press and wrap the piece of aluminum foil into a square shape and flatten and seal the sides and edges.

Step 5: Repeat the process until all the onions and potatoes are done.

Step 6: Place the aluminum covered package indirectly over the heat and keep it covered.

Step 7: Turn the package once and cook for 30 minutes.

Step 8: Serve and enjoy the grilled potatoes and onion while hot.

Spinach and Feta Pasta

Preparation Time: 25 minutes

Approximate Cooking Time: 15 minutes

Ready in: 40 minutes

Nutritional Value per Serving:

Calories: 451

Carbohydrates: 51.8 grams

Fats: 20.6 grams

Proteins: 17.8 grams

Cholesterol: 50 mg

Serving Size: Serves 4 people

Ingredients:

1 cup of fresh mushrooms, sliced

1 penne pasta, packaged (8 oz)

1 clove of minced garlic

1 pinch of red pepper flakes

2 tbsp of olive oil

½ a cup of onion, chopped

2 cups of packed spinach leaves

3 cups of tomatoes, chopped

8 oz of crumbled feta cheese

Salt and pepper for taste and seasoning

Directions

Step 1: Add salted water to a large pot and boil it.

Step 2: Add paste to the boiled water and cook until tender, drain the paste when done.

Step 3: While the pasta is cooking, take a large skillet, add some olive oil and place over medium – high heat.

Step 4: Add garlic and onion to the skillet and cook them until they turn golden brown in color.

Step 5: Throw in spinach, tomatoes and mushrooms in the skillet and add red pepper flakes, salt and pepper for seasoning purposes.

Step 6: Cook them for approximately 2 minutes, or until the spinach wilts and the tomatoes are well heated.

Step 7: Turn the heat down to medium and add some feta cheese and the pasta to the skillet.

Step 8: Cook them until all the ingredients are well incorporated and heated.

Step 9: Serve and enjoy the spinach and feta pasta.

Zucchini Grinders

Preparation Time: 20 minutes

Approximate Cooking Time: 30 minutes

Ready in: 50 minutes

Nutritional Value per Serving:

Calories: 339

Carbohydrates: 37.3 grams

Fats: 15.1 grams

Proteins: 16.9 grams

Cholesterol: 35 mg

Serving Size: Serves 4 people

Ingredients for Marinara Sauce:

2 cloves of coarsely chopped and peeled garlic

1 tbsp of olive oil

1 tsp of vinegar, red wine

1 tsp of sugar, white

1 tbsp of fresh basil, chopped

1 pinch of red pepper flakes, crushed

1 can of diced tomatoes, (14.5 oz)

Salt and pepper for taste and seasoning

Ingredients for Grinders:

2 medium cubed zucchini

1 pinch of red pepper flakes

1 tbsp of butter

1 ½ cups of mozzarella cheese, shredded

4 Italian or French split sandwich rolls, (6 inch)

Salt and pepper for taste and seasoning

Directions for Marinara Sauce

Step 1: Place a sauce pan filled with olive oil and place over medium heat.

Step 2: Add the basil, red pepper flakes and garlic to the pan and cook for approximately 2 minutes.

Step 3: Now add the vinegar, salt, pepper and sugar to the pan and stir regularly.

Step 4: Add tomatoes with their juices into the sauce pan and let it cook for approximately 15 minutes over low heat.

Step 5: Take the sauce pan over the heat and puree the mixture in a blender or food processor until it is smooth.

Directions for Grinders

Step1: Heat the oven beforehand to 175 degrees C (350 degrees F)

Step 2: Take a skillet, add some butter in it and leave to melt over medium heat.

Step 3: Add some zucchini to the skillet and cook it in the melted butter until it turns tender or brown in color.

Step 4: Sprinkle salt, pepper and red flakes on top for seasoning.

Step 5: Make sandwich rolls and add the zucchini mixture into them generously.

Step 6: Pour the marinara sauce mixture on top of the zucchini mixture in each roll.

Step 7: Wrap the sandwich rolls individually and cover them with aluminum foil.

Step 8: Put the sandwich rolls in the oven and bake for approximately 15 minutes.

Step 9: Serve and enjoy the zucchini grinders.

Ginger Veggie Stir-Fry

Preparation Time: 25 minutes

Approximate Cooking Time: 15 minutes

Ready in: 40 minutes

Nutritional Value per Serving:

Calories: 119

Carbohydrates: 8 grams

Fats: 9.9 grams

Proteins: 2.2 grams

Cholesterol: 0 mg

Serving Size: Serves 6 people

Ingredients:

1 tbsp of cornstarch

¾ cup of carrots, julienned

1 ½ cloves of crushed garlic

2 tbsp of soy sauce

¼ cup of divided vegetable oil

½ cup of snow peas

¼ cup of chopped onions

½ tbsp of salt

2 tsp of fresh ginger root, chopped and divided

1 small broccoli head, sliced into florets

2 ½ tbsp of water

Directions

Step 1: Take a large bowl and add some garlic, blend cornstarch, 2 tbsp of vegetable oil and 1 tsp of ginger, till the cornstarch is well dissolved.

Step 2: Add the green beans, carrots, broccoli and snow peas to the bow and mix them until lightly coated.

Step 3: Meanwhile, place a large skillet over medium heat and heat 2 tbsp of vegetable oil.

Step 4: Add the vegetables to the skillet and cook in the oil for approximately 2 minutes.

Step 5: Stir the vegetables regularly to prevent them from burning and some water and soy sauce to the mix as well.

Step 6: Add the salt, some onions and the remaining tsp of ginger to the skillet.

Step 7: Cook all of them until the vegetables are crisp on the outside yet tender inside.

Step 8: Serve and enjoy the ginger veggie stir-fry.

Swiss Chard with Garbanzo Beans and Fresh Tomatoes

Preparation Time: 10 minutes

Approximate Cooking Time: 15 minutes

Ready in: 25 minutes

Nutritional Value per Serving:

Calories: 122

Carbohydrates: 13.3 grams

Fats: 7.3 grams

Proteins: 3.2 grams

Cholesterol: 0 mg

Serving Size: Serves 4 people

Ingredients:

2 tbsp of olive oil

1 bunch of chopped and rinsed red Swiss chard

2 chopped green onions

1 sliced tomato

1 chopped shallot

½ juiced lemon

½ cup of drained garbanzo beans

Salt and pepper for taste and seasoning

Directions

Step 1: Place a large skillet over medium heat and heat the olive oil.

Step 2: Add the green onions and shallot into the skillet and cook for 3 – 5 minutes.

Step 3: Add some garbanzo beans with salt and pepper on top for seasoning and stir them properly to get the heat through them.

Step 4: Take another pan and add chard in it. Cook the chard until it is wilted.

Step 5: Add the tomato slices to the skillet and squeeze the lemon juice over the vegetables.

Step 6: Add some salt and pepper over the top for seasoning.

Step 7: Serve and enjoy the Swiss chard with garbanzo beans and fresh tomatoes.

Vegetarian Salads for Beginners!

When it comes to producing an outstanding salad dish, most people are found wanting. In fact several of the best cooks in the world have admitted that constructing and delivering a gorgeous salad is one of the most challenging things in cooking. Salads in a way define vegetarian cooking and you can't claim to be a vegetarian cooking if you can't whip up a nice scrumptious salad at the drop of a button.

A salad has to be light, yet contain different textures and flavors to really catch the attention of the person consuming it. You don't have to be a professional cook to learn how to make a good salad, it is in fact one of the simplest dishes you can make, and will be ready instantly with minimum preparation required.

Eating healthy goes hand in hand with eating light and nothing could be lighter than a nice healthy salad. Whatever the time or the occasion, a nice salad is definitely one dish which can be found on every menu anywhere in the world.

The salad recipes in this book are designed for people who want to learn how make a delicious salad in their kitchen. These restaurant quality vegetarian salads are sure to delight your family and friends, the next they come over at your place.

So why not try your hand at some of the most scrumptious vegetarian salads!

Chopped Black Bean-Avocado Salad

Preparation Time: 15 minutes

Approximate Cooking Time: 15 minutes

Ready in: 30 minutes

Nutritional Value per Serving:

Calories: 238

Carbohydrates: 24 grams

Fats: 14.5 grams

Proteins: 7 grams

Cholesterol: 0 mg

Serving Size: Serves 4 people

Ingredients:

2 tablespoons of lemon juice

1 tablespoon of mustard, whole – grain

1 cup of frozen or fresh corn

1 cup of rinsed and drained black beans, canned

1 diced avocado

2 tablespoon of olive oil

2 trimmed and thin sliced green onions

¼ cup of celery, diced

½ cup of cilantro, coarsely chopped

½ cup of sweet red pepper, diced

Directions

Step 1: Take a large bowl and add the mustard and lemon juice.

Step 2: Add some oil and whisk the mixture until it turns smooth.

Step 3: Throw the other ingredients and toss them gently to mix completely.

Step 4: Sprinkle some salt and pepper on top for seasoning.

Step 5: Serve and enjoy the chopped black bean-avocado salad.

Kale Salad with Pomegranate and Maple Pecans

Preparation Time: 15 minutes

Approximate Cooking Time: 25 minutes

Ready in: 40 minutes

Nutritional Value per Serving:

Calories: 216

Carbohydrates: 20 grams

Fats: 14 grams

Proteins: 7 grams

Cholesterol: 8 mg

Serving Size: Serves 6 people

Ingredients:

1 tablespoon of pure maple syrup

2 teaspoon of olive oil

¼ teaspoon of cayenne pepper

½ cup of pecan pieces

½ teaspoon of salt

2 tablespoons of balsamic vinegar

1 peeled and minced small shallot

2 tablespoons of olive oil, extra virgin

½ cup of pomegranate seeds

1 red apple, large, quartered, cored and sliced thinly

1 12 ounce bunch of Tuscan kale, sliced and deveined

Directions for Maple Pecan

Step 1: Preheat the oven to a temperature of 350 degrees F.

Step 2: Mix all the ingredients in a large bowl and toss until they are well coated.

Step 3: Place the ingredients on a baking sheet and bake for approximately 12 minutes.

Step 4: Take the ingredients out and let them cool.

Directions for Vinaigrette

Step 1: Combine all the ingredients together in a bowl.

Step 2: Whisk the entire ingredient together and ensure they are well coated.

Step 3: Sprinkle some salt and pepper for seasoning.

Directions for Salad

Step 1: Throw the Kale in a large bowl and gently pour the vinaigrette on top. Ensure that there is even covering of the vinaigrette.

Step 2: Add the pomegranate and apple to the kale and toss together to combine.

Step 3: Place some shaved Gouda and Maple Pecans on top of the dish.

Step 4: Serve and enjoy the kale salad with pomegranate and maple pecans.

Cucumber Salad with Peanut – Lime Vinaigrette

Preparation Time: 10 minutes

Approximate Cooking Time: 15 minutes

Ready in: 25 minutes

Nutritional Value per Serving:

Calories: 128

Carbohydrates: 5 grams

Fats: 11 grams

Proteins: 3 grams

Cholesterol: 0 mg

Serving Size: Serves 6 people

Ingredients:

1 tablespoon of lime juice

1 tablespoon of sesame oil, toasted

¼ teaspoon of salt

2 tablespoons of peanut oil

1 tablespoon of peanut butter

2 tablespoon of cilantro leaves

¼ cup of roasted peanuts, chopped

4 cucumbers, medium in size and sliced

Directions for Peanut – Lime Vinaigrette

Step 1: Add the peanut butter and lime juice in a bowl and whisk together to combine.

Step 2: Add the sesame and peanut oil and whisk until they are emulsified.

Step 3: Add some salt while emulsifying the vinaigrette.

Directions for Salad

Step 1: Place the cucumbers in layers of your choice on a plate.

Step 2: Sprinkle the cucumbers with the peanut – lime vinaigrette.

Step 3: Add some cilantro leaves and peanuts on top of the salad for taste.

Step 4: Serve and enjoy the cucumber salad with peanut – lime vinaigrette.

Egg and Veggie Salad with Dill Green Goddess Dressing

Preparation Time: 15 minutes

Approximate Cooking Time: 15 minutes

Ready in: 30 minutes

Nutritional Value per Serving:

Calories: 288

Carbohydrates: 26 grams

Fats: 14 grams

Proteins: 16 grams

Cholesterol: 233 mg

Serving Size: Serves 4 people

Ingredients:

10 purple potatoes, small and halved

16 orange cauliflowers, medium florets

4 cucumbers, Persian

5 eggs, large

1 tablespoon of balsamic vinegar

2 tablespoons of olive oil

¾ cup of Greek yogurt, nonfat

1 1/3 cup of fresh dill, chopped

1 bunch of fresh radishes, quartered and sliced

Directions

Step 1: Take a large vegetable steamer rack and place it in a pot in boiling water.

Step 2: Add some eggs to rack and encircle them with sliced potatoes.

Step 3: Place the cover on the pot and steam for approximately 10 minutes.

Step 4: Add some cauliflowers to the pot and steam for another 4 minutes until tender.

Step 5: Cut 1 cucumber and place it in the blender, add some vinegar, oil, 1/3 cup of dill and ¼ cup of yogurt with salt and pepper for seasoning blend until smooth.

Step 6: Add ½ cup of yogurt in a bowl and combine the blended mixture with the yogurt.

Step 7: Cut the remaining cucumbers into thin slices, and place them in a platter.

Step 8: Peel and quarter the eggs.

Step 9: Add the eggs cauliflowers, potatoes, radishes and cucumbers in a dish and sprinkle chopped dill on top for seasoning.

Step 10: Serve and enjoy the egg and veggie salad with dill green goddess dressing.

Conclusion – Cooking Vegetarian for Your Family!

Cooking for your family can be an absolute delight, and the recipes in this cookbook are designed to ensure that you have no problems in making delicious vegetarian food for your family, which can be prepared in an instant. It is important to look after the health and well being of your family, which is why we have seen a steady increase in the numbers of people who are considering going green in their choice of food.

Vegetarian food does not have to be tasteless or boring for that matter, and the recipes in this cookbook highlight that factor quite comprehensively. All the recipes are easy to make and require minimal time and effort in the kitchen on your part, which will no doubt be a source of delight for you.

Learning to cook vegetarian food can be fun for both you and your family. The recipes in the book are so simple that you can even invite your children to lend you a hand in the kitchen while making some of these dishes. Not only will that encourage the children to eat healthy food but will also create some beautiful memories for you and your family.

This vegetarian cookbook for beginners covers all the basic necessities which are required for amateur cooks to cook great vegetarian food. Have fun learning the recipes and making some delightful vegetarian dishes for your friends and family!

Printed in Great Britain
by Amazon

77924266R00032